C000279507

THREADING THE LIGHT

First published in 2019 by
The Dedalus Press
13 Moyclare Road
Baldoyle
Dublin D13 K1C2
Ireland

www.**dedaluspress**.com

ISBN 978 1 910251 59 1 (paperback)
ISBN 978 1 910251 58 4 (hardbound)

Dedalus Press titles are available in Ireland
through Argosy Books (www.argosybooks.ie) and in the UK
through Inpress Books (www.inpressbooks.co.uk).
Printed in Ireland by Digital Print Dynamics.

Cover image:
Detail of *Masts* by Craig Jefferson,
oil on panel, 23 x 30 cm (2016)
www.craigjefferson.com

The Dedalus Press receives financial assistance from
The Arts Council / An Chomhairle Ealaíon.

THREADING THE LIGHT

ROSS THOMPSON

DEDALUS PRESS

ACKNOWLEDGEMENTS

Acknowledgements and thanks are due to the following where a number of these poems, or versions of them, originally appeared:

The Bangor Literary Journal, The Blue Nib, Lagan Online, N.I. Screen 'Coast To Coast' Project, The Ogham Stone, One, Parhelion, Poetry In Motion Community Anthologies ('Matter', 'Resonance' and 'Find'), The Poetry Jukebox, The Remembered Arts Journal and *The Wild Word.*

I would also like to extend my gratitude for continuing encouragement, friendship and poetic camaraderie to Amy Wyatt Rafferty, Paul Rafferty, Andrew McAnally, the Arrell family, the Thompson family, Colin Dardis, Geraldine Dardis O'Kane, Craig Jefferson, David Braziel, Diane Morrow, Francis Jones, the Gamers, the Groggan Bears, Iain Campbell, Kevin Corstorphine, Linda Diffin, Maria McManus, Marie-Louise Muir, Matthew and Christine Cordner, Matthew Rice, Mel McMahon for his invaluable counsel, Michael and Laura Page, Mum and Dad, Nessa O'Mahony, Ray Givans, Stewart McCullough, Tory Campbell and of course my beloved Alison and Anna, without whom none of my endeavours would either be possible or worthwhile.

Special thanks to Pat Boran for his kindness, editorial guidance and above all for his faith in my writing.

Contents

ONE: IN PLACE

TWO: THE NEW WORLD

THREE: EYEING THE NEEDLE

FOUR: THE SILENT SHORE

FIVE: REACHING OUT

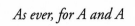

As ever, for A and A

One:
In Place

There Is Always A Lighthouse

The farmer's field, viewed from the single glazed
window of my childhood bedroom, was swathed

in downy darkness that fluttered, gently,
like stage curtains above drills of densely

packed soil. In fifteen second intervals,
an expanding circle of hibernal

light broke through a tear in the black fabric,
filling the dome with whispering cambric

then drained through the same distant interstice.
Again and again, the dark acquiesced

to the winking beam from a tapered tower
cut from Anglesey marble and ashlar,

and mounted with balcony and beacon.
The dark is strong but light never weakens.

July

By a horseshoe bay – calm, clean and ringed by green fields –
we squeeze the last drops from a postcard holiday

spent by the sea. Through glassy memory and dream,
time curves like liquid. You ebb towards me then flow

away. I tightrope walk the sharp teeth of the beach,
combing for treasure, weighing shells, measuring stones

and digging to Australia with my toy spade.
I can see you wringing your fingers and smoothing

down a pencil skirt whipped by the breeze. I can hear
you calling my name, warning me about cutting

my bare toes on crab claws … straying … breaking the chain …
then the film fades to black and the loop starts again.

Downhill

A flat, white disc of clean, smooth sand, tilted
slightly like a juggler's plate, yearns towards
a horizon, taut as wire, where Rathlin,
Scotland and the known universe balance

between human sight and the vanishing
point of infinite wisdom. God alone
could calculate the angle at which light
must slant to break through the prism of cloud

and make the troposphere glow like a jar
of pure acacia honey. Suffused
with amber, we are rendered angelic,
lightened of the burden of these fragile

bodies, floating like the lone ship caught in
slow motion further out on the ocean.

Sea

Faithful friend, endless, depthless, unfettered
     by time or distance, measured in hollowed
         hands, churning with pieces of eight, letters
    in bottles ... an untamed beast that bellows

and howls then turns calm as a lullaby,
     smooth and flat as polished glass, then crashes
         and spills, surges and breaks, shatters like ice,
    rolls, unfolds and unfolds again, washes

from costal spaces that boom and resound
     before receding but not depleting.
         This sea stretches from foot to ribs to crown,
    circles around the land before meeting

itself at a point that does not exist.
     Tuned to the pitch of a childhood refrain,
         the sea is sewn from memory and stitched
    with song. It roars in our bones like a flame.

Lifeblood

A blind needle finds a vein, and my crimson ink
goes pumping through a clear tube into the tin belly

of a greedy machine. It brings to mind sucking
milkshake up a curly straw while holidaying

as a boy on the Isle of Man. I remember
straying into the wrong chalet where a stranger

in polyester hooked up to some sort of gas
canister glanced at me over aviator

glasses – a real dead ringer for a serial
killer. I could not have got out of there faster.

I cannot answer why, while my lifeblood ferries
away to be tested for markers of cancer,

I am thinking about a random encounter
with an unknown figure who filled me with terror.

Magic Bullet

That day, two tall policemen in uniform
parked their jam sandwich and called at our door.
They asked my mum about a projectile

she had spied rocketing past her windshield
as she took the A2 back from Belfast.
She was driving when she noticed the glass

winking as the unknown object unseamed
the stitches that fixed the seen and unseen.
Had she not been slowing down to change lanes,

the thing would have lodged firmly in her brain
or ripped an extra hole in her gullet.
The police asked her to describe the "bullet" –

if that's what it was. No one was quite sure
why a gunman would take potshots at cars
on a carriageway, mid-afternoon lull

before rush hour and home time from school.
The policemen slurped their tea and asked,
"Did it glimmer like silver as it passed?

Did it hum or whistle? Like grass blades placed
in the snuffbox made when your thumbs are splayed
just wide enough to divine culling tunes?

Did it whine like a deflating balloon?
No, you say? It didn't sound like *that*?
Well, what then? A tremulous bandersnatch?

Are you sure it came from a gun? Maybe
a skilled bird hawked it from its fluted beak?
Perhaps a passing country rambler tripped,

fell forward and a sovereign ring slipped
from his finger at great speed? You don't think
so? Well, what then? Did it scurry or slink

like a squirrel foraging for loose nuts?
Was it like a water butt had frozen,
then cracked open, as if struck by Moses?

Come now, Mrs Thompson, try to focus.
Cast your mind back to the exact locus
where the missile nearly intersected

with your vehicle, where this suspected
metal slug emerged like a wild deer in
the heart of a forest: in this clearing,

this dappled grove, the truth is to be found.
You can chance on the proof there, on the ground
where it came to rest, the grass slightly singed.

Now tell me: what was the mystery thing
you saw today? Can you recall the word?
Yes. Yes, I thought so. It was just a bird."

Pest House

for Helen

A month off school: one long and humid afternoon
quarantined inside a crushed emerald bedroom.

Head laid on damp cloth, he babbled to Test Card F
while a fresco of Death drew itself like hot breath

on a winter pane. Close by, a plague stone, well stocked
with vinegar and prayer, warned of measles, mumps, pox

and whooping cough. Doctors, in oilcloths and perfumed
beaks, called at his charnel to administer blooms

of treacle and arsenic where this fallen bird, dazed
after crashing against a glassy palisade,

muttered nursery rhymes and memento mori
while his sister placed plastic pennies on his eyes.

Illuminated

for Iain Campbell

Exasperated after a good hour
of checking the green flex, testing each bulb
to ensure it was anchored in the wire
by giving it a righty-tighty turn,

hoping that each deft twist of his fingers,
each digital somersault, would unlock
the light that was blocked by a stubborn fault
in one of the unlit electric wicks,

my father gave in, dropped the broken string
and moaned that he had lost the way of things.
The tree was as dark as it would have been,
standing unfelled in the wood where we chopped

it down, breath frosting my lips as he taught me
to grip the axe, the right angle to make
a notch without the trunk pinching the blade,
and how to read the moon's light as a guide.

Postscripts

I remember those sighs, deep as a glacier,
streaming from her as she traced one slender index
finger over embossed font in the newspaper.

As if reading braille or brushing away dust flecks,
she caressed the lettering with maternal care.
Whether capital, lower, straight or circumflex,

each character felt the press of her tenderness
and the comforting ellipse of her fingertips.
Eyes glistering with damp mascara, she addressed

the class after composing herself, the *clacks* and *clicks*
of her heels a rhythmic beat for the weekly test
in conjugating verbs and rote-learnt mnemonics.

Some years later, I discovered that my teacher
had once delivered English to green police cadets
who bore no love for iambic pentameter

or feminine rhyme. Many met untimely deaths
in the bleak eighties, silenced by detonator
or armalite, now all but forgotten except

in weekly obituaries written in black
and traced by my teacher, hoping to undo fact.

Struck

My grandfather was a big man who filled
a room with fables that caught the true wind
like a coloured mainsail and set our course
for South America: me on his knee,

manning the wheel; him at stern, bellowing
encouraging words as we braved a storm
that rose up from below. The kraken's tail
whipped our ship. Lightning forked the mast. A thread

of ice drew a dividing line between
two annexed sides of his body. A whole
bank of circuit breakers broke, went to sleep
and never awoke. Slumped in his armchair,

he shrunk smaller than a vanishing star.
His mouth, now an adit to a collapsed
mine, whispered bits of words that failed to tell
how far his mind was torn by civil war.

Thereafter, our ship remained locked in port.

Threads

Mid 1980s, and I spend most days
petrified by the threat of the world's end:
a vision of a thin, quicksilver blade,
powered by fission, tapering from white flames,

hanging in the sky, drawing a thick line
across pitched triangular rooftops
of red brick detached houses just like mine,
and the shimmering smiles of high street shops

ready to spit out melting mannequins
through molten glass as a shockwave flattens
every town dotted along the Ulster Way.

I am a very timid child. Most days
pulse with Soviet fear of the whole sphere
being cleared of all living things apart

from one: the nuclear fug disappears,
and I am left behind on a razed earth,

alone and too weak to pick up the threads.

Returns

for Dad

A golden bottle, cool and smooth as a singing stone,
rests in my infant palm, wet with condensation
straight from the fridge. I know the ridges and trade name
as I have downed enough flutes of Brown Lemonade
to launch a thousand ships. A kindly uncle sneaks
them from the bottling plant at the end of each week:
Cream Soda, Red Kola and Orange Crush.
I love it when, uncapped, chilled fizz can rush
into the mouth: a bolt of cold nectar,
a slug of brambly Sarsaparilla
that hits the back of the throat like a ghost
train run off the rails. The smooth syrup coats
my windpipe on the way down south, dances
on my tongue and the gap where my tonsils
once hung. We chug bottles dry and pretend
they are full of beer, tilted up on end
to be kissed mouth to mouth like an angel's
trumpet. I am lightheaded and grateful,
less so for the noxious cigarettes
my uncle smokes, and therefore for the debt
he cannot repay. Once empty, we bring
back the bottles in bags of light that sing
a song of what they used to hold, returned
for chocolate money that we had not earned.

The Bad Boys' House

On Sunday afternoons you took long walks
with your parents by the open air pool,
outdoor gospel pews, smuggler's cove, fun park
and those leafy avenues where you stole
conkers. You felt you were an impostor
in this closed off realm of old world grandeur.
One street was marked by a dark house: a swear
word scrawled on a kerb that caught your young eye
and made you flush. Your mum said it was where
bad boys were sent when disobedient.
You, clean-living and innocent as snow,
thought of those bad boys at school who lied, stole
and doled out beatings without a second
thought: dead arms, "Red Hands of Ulster", lashes
with the wetted ends of tightly-bound towels.
A litany of welts and brash bruises
that cut right to your bones: a reminder
of who owned you; how your home was never
too far away from the reach of bad boys
inured to using knives and words and stones.
And that fear: what if you were ever caught
doing something you should not? Or accused
with a charge that was patently untrue?
You would not last a day in that borstal.
They would chew you into tiny morsels.

Blue Lamp Disco

The assembly hall was all biz the day
the police came to talk to us about drugs.
The boys called a ceasefire on their scarf fight
re: Spandau Ballet and Duran Duran,
and the girls quit their handstand contest
to come inside to sit in neat bean rows,
tempted by the prospect of a disco.
A policeman shaped like a lower case **b**
warned us of the dangers of cigarettes,
alcohol and someone called Mary Jane –
she must have attended a different school.
After the ganching, one of the other
chaps in uniform pushed a big button
and a double punch drum machine whammy
of Falco and Baltimora juddered
cups of diluted juice as we ventured
our best imitation of the moonwalk,
lawnmower and cabbage patch. Everyone
danced as if their lives depended on it.
Everyone, that is, except that lonely
boy whose birthday party I attended
two years before – I bought him a Batman
doll and got sugar-spangled on top hats
and Coca Cola but he retreated
to the corner and cried for his mother.
Years after, he ran away from the town's
gladiatorial grammar, eloping
to England one summer with an online
lover, much older. The police visited
again. They delivered a stern warning
about a different danger. No dancing,
no drum machines and no synthesisers.

Boutade

An hour past bedtime, and I was still halfway down
a rabbit hole of videogames and comics,
curtains bedecked with cartoon BMX riders
not yet drawn, the black window a magic mirror
that gave back the ghosts of us: the flickering plane
of the cathode ray and my teenage self, huddled
close to the miniature set, volume turned down
so my parents would not detect my manoeuvres
and discover the carelessly discarded pile
of homework books lying unopened on the floor.
I had just cracked *Super Metroid* when the window
shook in its jamb, bending inwards like rain speckling
a spiderweb, causing my reflection to warp
then snap into shape, followed by a distant thud,
like a neighbour tumbling down some stairs, then a just
audible cacophony of panicky bells
and sirens, as if echoing within a well
dug deep into the earth. I knew enough to know
that a bomb – maybe incendiary, perhaps
Semtex – had ripped out the heart of the town.
Other cities had been attacked and we were next.

The following day, I took a walk after school
to ground zero, Lower Main Street, where half-vanished
buildings hung like carcasses in an abattoir,
charred parking bays homed roofless cars and the distinct
scent of fear and betrayal choked the dusty air.

Sylvia

It was meant to be a spot of harmless fun.
You hid beneath your bed when you heard your mum
come calling you to hurry downstairs for tea,
then go falling through the house like a coin

inside a fruit machine, pinging from room to room,
clanging across floor tiles and slamming doors,
calling your name,
                    calling your name,
                                        calling your name,
her songbird voice growing more loud and shrill

with each futile search and unanswered plea.
At one point, her slippered feet twitched within reach
of your retreat but they swiftly disappeared.
You lay in the dust motes and Lego pieces,

so very pleased with your prank, and listened
to her unclick the telephone receiver
from its cradle and ask for the police.
Still, you did not emerge, choosing instead

to play dead, lying tranquil while the house
filled with neighbours, their voices spilling into
your cell like water from a well. A rope
of sunlight lowered between patterned blinds,

frayed thin then ceased reaching in, and the room
was leased to darkness. You dozed and floated
a breath above the floor below's lightbulbs.
It rang with the hubbub of relatives

and friends readying torches, waterproof
jackets and laminated maps. You dreamt
of sneaking into the kitchen, making
a grand entrance by guldering, "Surprise!"

and seeing the startled look in their eyes
before they all would laugh, clap and wrap
you in their arms. But you stayed where you were,
curled up on your side while the window frame

flashed blue and white, and your poor mother cried
and cried
                    and cried
                                        and cried
                                                            and cried

and cried.

I'm On Fire

Her student housing single bed mattress
    held not quite enough room for both of us.

Quotation marks on the divided line
    with the base of her spine pressed against mine,

we lay trembling on the edge of the cliff,
    listening to music with the lights off.

Yearning to reach my hand into the dark
    and start a riot of Halloween sparks

but too timid to move a single muscle,
    I stayed rigid, bent at a right angle,

counting quavers, minims and semibreves
    then uncurled and made excuses to leave.

On the way home, I paused to catch my breath
    and watched lit windows offer silhouettes.

Eidetically

I can still picture the scene, clear enough to feel
and taste,

playing out in high definition, as if real,
not yet erased,

in spite of dropping it like cats in a jute sack
into a great lake.

The memory is too stubborn to be submerged:
it was late

as we walked to the Old Town, my arm looped around
her waist,

placed high above Waverley station, her teasing
and tempting fate,

climbing railings, defying gravity, asking
in her singsong way

if I had ever considered jumping. She had.
She was not afraid,

she said, to throw herself carelessly from the bridge
into the fray

but she refrained and her life continued, happy
and unchanged.

My mind assigned her a different timeline: plunging
like a stray

angel, suspended above a glass terminus,
an arced skyway

of Victorian steel that could break her body
like falling rain.

She may not have jumped but the echo of her words
still resonates.

Roman Candle

for Quentin

Remember that tall glass of bile: a gangly goon
in a biker jacket we met while sojourning
in the university halls of residence.
His favourite pastime was tormenting those students
who beat a path different to his own – mostly
those wasters immersed in the *beaux arts*. The scent
of marijuana wafting off his unwashed clothes
suggested a dozy bent for pacifism
but the truth was he was uncouth and wound tighter
than the fibres in a bishop's mitre. This gent
had enrolled much later in life, and to that end
had built up considerable resentment.
He first took umbrage when he spotted *The Bible*
poking out of my luggage. In the dining hall,
over a plate of potato croquettes, he said
he hated my faith and then gave me the stink-eye
for my choice to not drink wine, pints or "green monster"
shots made from goodness knows what with a dash of rum.
He threatened to dip me in oil like a tapered
wick and set me on fire, just like how they treated
Christians in the Colosseum. But this tough talk
made him a liar: he scarpered to his perfumed sanctum
where he listened to death metal and swung weak fists
and cursed at a God in whom he did not believe.
On a rare trip to the Union, that sepulchral
building heaving with the scent of cheap burgers,
yeast and desperation, he came for a pilgrim
or a patsy to use as a plaything. Devoid
of lions that needed feeding, he seized my throat
and offered to pin me to a cross. I refused

to turn the other cheek. I socked him in the teeth
and taught him to bleed before hiding in the crowd.
I was not proud but a victim of that old rule:
bullies still exist, even after leaving school.

Crop Circles

Breaking all codes of transgress, you sidled
through the hedge, your breath dampening the cloth
of your balaclava. A moonlit field
of expectant wheat bowed before your feet.

You trod softly, carefully. Parallel
tractor tracks provided a path without
a record of your trespass. Carrying
planks, rope and spade, you slunk to the centre

of purring grain, following the steps mapped
out on a detailed scale drawing on graph
paper: a geometric curlicue
of plumb lines and saucer shapes.

You set to work, marking out the design
by laying out tools on top of soft crops
then pressing them with your feet so the field
yielded to the diagram imprinted

on your mind's eye. When you were done, first light
illuminated dew on broken grass
as a warning to make your way back home.
The following day, the local paper

reported strange overnight occurrences
with pictorial proof: a bamboozled
farmer standing in a circular brand
of dead wheat, shoulders raised in disbelief.

Orpheus

A glowing throat of pale blue flowers. A corridor,
pinpricked by blinking lights, stretched lengthwise like a sigh
to a vanishing point and an exit of sorts.

A fading taper, drawn back to the living land.
A thin beam along which you sleepwalk every night.
A dead zone, a proving ground, a cartoon gangplank

of vinyl tiles on which two overlaid timelines,
carved out by your avatar winding his way up
from dank hospital ward to neon exit sign,

resonate like a tuning fork pitched to the key
of E minor. A path of bitter cups
of burnt coffee before one last retreat.

You hold your breath until you make it clear.
Glancing back, you see yourself disappear.

Narkosläkare

Milky film cradles my skin just below
the jawline. His hands are soft but still firm
and fragranced with apples and lavender.

Saltpepper wings poke out from a neat cap.
He places a dry conch over my mouth,
surgical mask rippling like cellophane

as he instructs me to count down from ten.
Syrup, warm as soil, siphons through my veins.
The cold steel beneath my back is a bed

of swan feathers, a damp sandbank yielding
to my weight. A steep field dotted with blood
poppies spreads in all directions beneath

a sea of noxious green. At the apex,
like a golden sun, the Easter Island
head of the anaesthetist keeps vigil,

holding me in snoozy purgatory.
A strange thought: the last face I remember
will not belong to my earthly father.

True Faith

A balmy evening in August,   coasting
through the city centre to meet   old friends
for cold drinks and chat, windows up to keep
in the heat, indie music off   for once,

the only sounds are the engine   humming
and the buffering of tarmac   beneath
four wheels, summer light shimmering like gold
through leaf-laden trees lined along bright streets

as if the world was held inside   the hand
of a skilled jeweller, its value   appraised,
rotated to reveal every   detail
and grace note. This brave world is born again.

You hear your name being spoken   gently,
soft as linen, from far away   and close
by: a voice that is not female   or male
or even human, welling both   inside

and out, telling you to slow down   and *stop*.
You tap the brakes. The car obeys.   A cry,
panicked and shrill, rings out across the street.
A mother, arms outstretched as if   pleading,

watches her child running into   the space
where your car would be had you not   listened.

Bangor

I woke up this morning with a song in my ear,
ringing like the buoys in the harbour, by the pier
where teenagers ride their bikes during hot summers.
Foolish souls take diving headers into water
colder than the interior of the outdoor
baths, long since demolished, where folk once swam while war
raged overseas. The song rang through tall trees, the aisles
of Castle Park from Abbey bell to broken dial
carved from slate that, when it was complete, could divine
the sun and moon. It surged strongly like a ley line
or the shared pulse in warm arms sharing embraces
so heart can beat against fellow hearts in places
near and dear where a fire burns in an open hearth
and parting glasses are always ready to charge.
The song rang inside totem poles in Crawfordsburn,
chiming between rail bridge struts where lovers adjourn
on humid evenings when the air tastes sharp and sweet
with honeysuckle and stones salted from the sea.
It whispered close to the coastal path, inside coves,
the ghost of a bandstand to Queen's Parade where droves
of tourists flocked for pokes of Italian ice cream
in a post-war heyday jet stream where the daydream
of France, Spain and Disney World was yet to be made
a reality. The song continued to play,
refusing to fade, in playgrounds and pedaloes
shaped like swans, walled garden, canon and tremolo
of ship masts in the marina. It resounded
in brick, glass and ground, and I was dumbfounded,
in awe of such energy, the magnetic force
that draws us home like sailboats on a watercourse.

Two:
The New World

The Sheridan Theatre (1937)

after Edward Hopper

Forsaking the grisaille world of Greenwich,
       I took shelter in the technicolour
movie palace. For less than half a buck
       I eavesdropped on Mae West and Cary Grant,

Snow White, Galahad and Marlene Dietrich.
       There, cradled by the balustrade's wooden
parabola, I could dress in someone
       else's glad rags, freshly sugarcoated

by the dichroic beam that renamed me
       Greta, Jean, Carole, Marlene ... marked woman,
gangster's moll, the belle of Saratoga,
       my silhouette projected on the screen

where, from the balcony to the cheap seats,
       folk were raptured by candy and soda,
elevated from the Great Depression
       and this downmarket nickelodeon,

broadcasts of Nazis and impending war.
       All week long I was on loan to my drudge
job as an office drone but the stretch of
       Saturday and Sunday was spent binging

on movies in my *theatrum mundi*,
       a new deal where anything could happen,
where time stood still, and where my screwball dreams
       were never too outlandish to be real.

The Projectionist's Hands

Slow but insistent as rain, the projectionist
makes his way to the magic booth, past the disused

piano, the lovely young girl selling taffy,
and the owner's daughter sweeping up confetti.

He pads over carpets deep and red as the Nile
in that biblical one by Cecil B. DeMille,

and slips slim hands into cotton gloves, whisper thin,
to stop his skin from sticking to delicate film.

He unlocks the box sealed with asbestos and wax
to hold in fire should the nitrate reels ever catch

alight and burn up like napalm. Print is brittle
and must be handled with care: the slightest spittle

or dust makes it flare like sulfur mustard. He racks
twin projectors, gently lifts out the strip, and tracks

it on the spool. Light fills the auditorium.
Shadows dance and swoon inside the proscenium.

The audience gasps. Little do they know or care
how stock shoots across white hot carbon rods. He hears

it whirr, waits for cue dots, black circles marked with ink;
gauges the sweet spot with fingers dusted with zinc.

Cigarette Girl

It was never supposed to turn out this way:
a facsimile of discarded scraps,
a palimpsest, a half-remembered cliché.

She was bright, sparky, pretty enough to be sprayed
on the side of warplanes so how did she wind up
wearing a pillbox hat and holding a tray

of light-up yo-yos, roses, chewing gum
and *Home Run* cigarettes, faking a smile
for handsy gangsters boasting about running rum

through the Canadian pipeline? Their well-thumbed
come-ons made her gag as she walked the aisles
of The Ruby Moon Club, legs sharp as shotguns,

a dab of Coco Chanel behind each knee.
Once, she flew away, like Dorothy or Dahlia,
from the backwards town they named that disease

after, all smiles, fizzing with hopes and dreams,
and later reappeared, floating like Ophelia
up the Hudson River, sparkling in the sunbeams.

Chaplinitis

Many years later, after fame and fortune waned,
I entered a contest under an assumed name,

where droves of hopeful lookalikes for you-know-who
congregated by night at a vaudeville revue

in a fleapit theatre just off the Sunset Strip.
There were countless variations of counterfeit

hat, cane, garb and bow-legged gait: every homage
replete with a version of that awful moustache,

each toothbrush more hideous than the last.
Finally, when the judges' vote was cast,

they bestowed first prize on an imposteur,
a regular bona fide Martin Guerre,

but I, deemed unconvincing in the role
for which I was universally known,

limped in, the story goes, a dismal twelfth.
I was not deemed worthy to play myself.

Arisaig, 1973

It took the villagers nearly eight years of graft
to lay umpety yards of cable and erect a mast

to catch signals broadcast from Skye to the rough bounds,
one of the remotest black spots in the Highlands.

Those who owned spirit lanterns by Mitsubishi
could sample the rough magic of the BBC:

the Watergate scandal and the Vietnam War,
Call My Bluff, The Clangers, J. Fred Buzhardt, *Z Cars*

and sitcoms, Patrick Moore and a solar eclipse,
Typhoon Ruth, Billie Jean King trouncing Bobby Riggs,

the Soup Dragon, Picasso's death and Wounded Knee,
Skylab, Humpty and Presley live in Hawaii,

Yoffy, Deep Throat, the dark side of the moon, *Colditz,*
Pan's People, Comet Kohoutek and *Crystal Tipps.*

Some folks said that it would be a bad influence
while others tuned into *The Old Grey Whistle Test.*

The Tonic, 1982

Lucid dreams of red brick, glowing snowcrete,
lambent glass and gold panelled Art Deco
borrowed from Monte Carlo casinos,
are repurposed on a suburban street,
welcoming folk in with a grandiose sweep
of carved marble steps and hoarding boasting
The Empire Strikes Back. Once through the marquee:
a spree of newfangled gizmos roasting
nuts, romance, chittering ticket kiosks,
Compton organ with the teeth of a shark,
pretty usherettes each toting a box
of fresh fruit ices or piercing the dark
with switchless torches, spooling quicksilver
to a red velvet chair – the premier
spot in-between Gatling gun projector
and candescent screen, where a lumière
beam of blue, white and green gilds the whole room,
turning silhouettes aureate, eclipsed,
then solar with trombones at full volume.

The film begins. I am at once transfixed.

It ends too soon. The lure of video
holds folk hostage. The Tonic, devalued,
closed down, gutted by fire, a cameo
of the town's past … and I am gutted too.

Olympia Splendid '66

for Christopher Murray

They found the room at the top of crooked stairs,
sealed and forgotten, hidden behind a partition

of cross stitch and screen prints. A *pop*, then a *hiss*
when they worked the obstruction free, and the loft

pooled with buttery light. They were not greeted
by cobwebs, pipistrelles and lungfuls of fusty dust

but by a phalanx of gleaming typewriters, ready
to receive eager fingers, pockmarked by engagement

rings and cigarette burns, each platen waiting
to be fed a crisp sheet of blank paper, each ribbon

impatient to tongue words onto the page, each
shelf empty ... apart from one: a vintage device,

midnight black with ebony keys, nursing a solitary
folio, yellowed slightly at the corners, bearing

the same touch-typed phrase, over and over and over:
I ask nothing of you ... only that you love me.

The Trapeze Artist

All those hours spent in my father's gymnasium,
    practising pirouettes above a swimming pool,
burdened me with vertigo and a bruised abdomen
    but I would not exchange it for all of the jewels

in India. Snapped limbs, burst blood vessels and calloused
    palms were milestones on the hard road to The Winter
Circus, nestled in the bustling heart of Paris.
    I was a wild exotic bird, satined and feathered,

shooting between Corinthian columns like a bead
    on an abacus, upside down with heart in mouth,
turning tricks with trapeze tucked behind my knees
    with no harness or mattress if things went south.

Great men wrote songs about my shows at the Alhambra,
    where I wowed London diners with penny rolls, hocks
and whips before vanishing into the sharp penumbra
    and falling foul of an outbreak of smallpox.

New pleasures arrived: the cancan, ballet, parlour
    magic, the Colonna Troupe, men who claimed to talk
to the dead, dancing bears, a smidgen of opera,
    a theurgist who plucked light bulbs from their stalks

then swallowed them so they glowed within his exposed chest.
    None of these shysters came close to grazing the stars
as I did when bravely launching from the crow's nest,
    gracing the gap before the cutaway bar.

Remnants

A long weekend spent sightseeing around Paris,
hammered after peach Bellinis from Aux Folies,
we wobbled from Sacré-Cœur to the Grand Palais,
Notre-Dame, the Louvre and the Musée d'Orsay

until we found a trapezium of indents
carved near where la Roquette no longer pressed against
the city skyline: five rectangles on the ground
where a guillotine, built by a German renowned

for making harpsichords, had once unencumbered
criminals of their skulls. The headless dead numbered
in the hundreds, and ghosts of traitors were revealed
all the way from the saltire to the breaking wheel.

I pictured your husband at your home in Quebec
and felt the crescent blade whispering on my neck.

Domino Day

Fingers numb from squeezing round-tip tweezers,
a team of ninety master builders placed
the final of five million tiles, levered
delicately into each artery

of rainbow-coloured polyforms: fifteen
miles of interlocking cascades arranged
with sole intent of knocking them over
again to make a sound like falling rain.

It took the guts of two months to lay out
the display inside an airtight warehouse
once reserved for the storage of seaplanes,
hermetically sealed to shut out stray birds

or gusts lest the whole blessed array fall
in a heap before the build was complete.
The trick to placing dominoes: the gap
between each one, a pinch of air wider

than a synapse and thinner than a spark,
measured, as if by Rube Goldberg, to start
a chain reaction and let gravity do the work.
But the risks are high: a nervy digit,

loose breath or dead tile can scupper the whole
show. No erupting volcano, dancing
semibreves or tessellating portraits
of Lionel Richie. Picture the panic

when a spider, spindle-limbs and dust-drop
body, was picked up by security
cameras, gingerly creeping across
the lintels of a microform Stonehenge,

placing tiny tufted claws on a ring
of gunmetal grey trilithons before
slow-walking into a diorama
of a fully functional amusement

park: dodgems, roller coaster and log flume
all in danger of launching too early
and breaking the chain of plastic fractals
and glass Fibonacci spirals. The team

waited with baited breath as the spider,
microscopic cilia fluttering
all over its body, perched on the roof
of a reduced Taj Mahal, where it spun

a web between minarets. This thread spread
outwards, rounder and fatter, becoming
a ball, then a nest, then a catcher's mitt,
then a melon, then an inflatable

beach ball, expanding wider and taller
until the entire hall was filled. The team
and all their carefully laid dominoes
were web-bound, where they remain enveloped

to this day, neither falling nor failing.

Seelonce Mayday

1.

Wall Street. Early morning. Already, the bear pit
is a cloud of white noise: the stock exchange
chanting algorithms and frenzied semaphore
of traders one scalp away from a heart attack.

I quit the floor, make for the security doors,
the bangarang of junked-up whale hunters ringing
in my ears. Outside, the city is an ant farm
of sunlit glass: a blitzkrieg of pedestrians

pummelling past, coffee cups and iPhones in hand,
barely pausing for the klaxon to grant passage
across a river of traffic filtering close
by like binary code. I hail a cab. It sails

up to the kerb like a luxury yacht. I make
the airport in thirty nought nought. Baggage handling. ·
Customs. Duty Free. Boarding. I am fast asleep
before the wheels leave the ground. I dream without sound.

2.

I am spat clean out of sleep when a drop-down tray
hits my knees. The plane leaps like a salmon
from a stream as a sheet of lightning shears
off one wing. For a breath there is only

confusion, a scrabbling to comprehend
what has happened and what is happening,

quite how the man beside me, a farmer
from Skokie, Illinois, could be alive

then immediately dead; how another
could lose his head when a loose suitcase shoots
through the shell-shocked cabin like a pellet
from a catapult; how a financial

executive, who has spent the journey
pounding consecutive appletinis,
could evaporate into fine, golden dust
as his soul spears out of his firebombed shell.

3.

The sole survivor. The miracle girl,
they will say. Against all odds, the woman
who, by an act of God, does not perish
in a freak accident that spent the lives

of 142 other
passengers and crew but is left clutching
onto a shard of severed fuselage,
sunburnt with lungs full of salt and jet fuel,

no injuries bar a fractured pelvis
and a broken wrist, adrift for days
before I will be discovered halfway
between Madagascar and Atlantis.

A media plaything. The missing piece
from twelve dozen eulogies, the human
interest in an award-winning movie
who makes it home safe and stays lost at sea.

A Sort Of Revelation

John Ruskin – you may well have heard of him –
sat at his desk with a sole thought niggling
his mind like a stubborn splinter anchored
in a carpenter's finger: *how he could
describe clouds.* To date he had found the words
for the gentle way that gossamer light
fell across the landscape at dawn, or how
a twig is a tree in miniature
but clouds … well, they eluded him. Unsure
of how to shape language to cloak a mass
of vapour and water, he got himself
into quite the twist trying to account
for fog and mist, and nearly rent his mind
asunder in search of a fitting phrase
for how the air tastes before and after
a plague of thunder. He could not find rest
imagining that the heavens above,
the firmament beneath whose weight the world
is pressed, might resemble a woman's flesh,
and how, as soon as he pinned down the shape
of a roaring lion or a hare tearing
through a meadow at dawn, the clouds had gone.
Like thought, clouds conceal more than they reveal.

Asleep In The Back Seat

for Mel McMahon

Tartan wool, the distinct smell of Scotland,
lightly grazed my skin as I lay full stretch
along the back seat of our rental car,
the rockabye chugging of wheels against

highway a few feet beneath my bare cheek,
road stretched like dreams through the still Toronto
evening. I was just barely aware
of the humid air inside the cabin,

thankfully free from my dad's usual choice
of long-players by Nana Mouskouri,
Max Boyce and hateful pan pipe renditions
of 'Hey Jude' and 'God Only Knows', clearing

the channel for my mum's voice to ring through
the fog of sleep: an old music hall tune
half-remembered yet clear and true, catching
streetlights dancing above my haloed brow.

Three:
Eyeing the Needle

Anatidae

Christmas,
and all day long it was raining stair rods.

After supper,
it had eased to an insistent mizzle:

a gentle soaking
of angel breath and fairy light tears.

Hopped up
on marzipan, chestnuts and cabin fever,

I dragged
my reluctant dog to the park

through a fleece
of translucent mist enfolding

nightshade play park
and bedlam birdcages in fenny quiet.

On the pond,
two courting swans moved through the brume

like pencil lines
across tracing paper or shadows on shoji.

The Happiness Matters

i.m. Elliott Smith

The rain is not taking the time to rain.

The sky is a ruptured turnpike, weeping
onto comfortable suburbia,

streaking bedroom windows with glaucoma,
lying heavily upon the town's bones.

Suddenly, blindsided by memories:

1.

pedalling my bike on country roads,

trying to outrun the raincloud moving
like a mothership across the landscape,

expanding, and dark as melanoma,
ready to unleash its pungent contents

onto its fearful acolyte racing
home along a jet stream of waning light.

2.

watching your concert in a tinderbox
venue in Glasgow, walls damp with hot sheets

of sweat and beer, you appearing onstage
to the clamour of song requests and cheers,

smiling and joking, in no way showing
the black cloud dangling above like a sword.

It hurts my heart too much to think of it.

Infinity

i.m. Pete Wedderburn

Take a straight line, a breadthless length of breath
and joy, then remould the shape, lemniscate.

See how it curves in and out of itself ...
an infinite loop that recedes from sight

then arcs around, a shooting star, tracing
a pathway of matter and transverse light.

Look closely, and you might spy me, waving
back as we rocket past: two birds in flight,

parallel for a moment, an eye-blink
on the timeline of the universe's great

sprawl. We dissipate, not like leaves or snow
but dreams that linger though they might appear

to evaporate. The day and the night
are divided by the slightest margin,

and the sound of an echo is still heard
long after the ring of the parting word.

Promettre

I promised you a peach – your favourite.
The thought of the fruit's flesh, sweet like summer
rain, wet like meadow dew, eased your dry mouth.

But I could not find you a peach. Instead,
I gave you the word: *peach*. Smooth and tasteless,
it clung to your tongue till you spat it out.

I promised you a storm, to lay you down
on a bed of squall in a clifftop shack.
Instead, I gave you the word: *storm*. You closed

your eyes but you could not picture yourself
clutching onto rock for dear life. We hoped
for hail and fire and gale but all we had

were words, calm as a cornfield, safe as love,
and none of these things were ever enough.

Honeysuckle

You read somewhere that you could snap
      a honeysuckle flower from the vine,
tear it in two, and taste nectar beading
      on the lip of the exposed wound.

You sprinted to the garden, where you found
      a bush thrumming with hummingbirds,
and weighted with vibrant purple blooms
      but when you tried to conjure sugar

onto your tongue, you could not taste honey.
      You were left with the bitter tang of pollen
and a handful of broken corollas.
      Another time, you held a tropical conch

against your ear, hoping to hear the voice
      of choristers washing in and out
of the aperture. But as the shell's mouth kissed
      your cheek, you could not hear the sea.

The Wild Hunt

for Alison

A driving holiday to the Scottish Highlands,
and on the way to Skye the road narrows and turns
serpentine, rattling the car as it coils around
the side of a fierce mountain rising from patchwork

earth like a jagged blade. The day is still and strange.
Magic light spills across the sweep of heather, gorse,
thistle and rock, blessing savage terrain with wind
bristling with rain as we ascend towards Heaven.

For a moment we are lightheaded – the laughing
gas of clouds, the bubblegum popping of warm ears
– and then we are lowered down, as if through a hole
in the burnt clay roof of the sky, where a forest,

thick as teal velvet curtains, draws back to reveal –
I hammer the brakes. A majestic stag, chewing
nonchalantly on wads of grass, stands galvanised,
antlers winking like the crown of a golden king,

flank shimmering, blocking our path to the alien
landscape beyond. He trains us with his ancient eye
for a breathless age then stands aside to allow
passage over the threshold between the two worlds.

Sometimes, as I fall asleep, I catch a fleeting
glimpse of that same eye, wet and filmy as rock pools:
the moon's oculus breaking the gap in the blinds,
permitting me entry into my borrowed dreams.

Skye

A miracle of engineering, a magic trick,
a bridge cantilevered between mainland and isle
to a remote part of the country growing wild
with a tapestry of heather moor, thistle and gorse.
Taking this trip is like zapping back in time:
a few beats from Portree, where lobster and langoustine
are as plentiful as manna, we drive out towards
a Pictish landscape of agate and marcasite,
home to countless guillemot and red deer. The air
tastes fresh as the sea. The ground throbs with rivulets
and streams coursing from the belly of Sgùrr nan Gillean.
On Sunday, we join in worship with islanders
raising palms and reciting psalms to the Saviour.
We are welcomed for dinner by complete strangers.
We break bread and crack open carafes of blood red wine.
Chat flows like water from the rock struck by Moses's staff.
After, we head out into the dark, where distant headlamps
wash over the shapes of roosting birds and sleeping trees.
We retire to the solitary B & B resting
on the estuary that gives back all the light
of the moon, and we spoon in a queen size bed that allows
us to be different people for a few stolen
moments, far removed from the pressure and the din
of the city from which we fled and tried to forget.

Cordyline

for Robert Arrell

Potbound when we first stumbled upon it,
almost choked by its own roots in a dark
and disused corner of the forgotten
garden, we carefully scooped the wilted

shrub out of its ceramic shell, taking
care not to damage its thirsty, brittle
lobes and umbels that hung low like tattered
flags. You slowly disentangled the ball

of yellow wool spiralled beneath its base,
carried it to a puddle of gold
and immersed it deep within the warm soil,
where, fired by magic, it thrived with new life.

For the next decade your daughter (my wife)
and I barely noticed time slipping by,
and all the while the Cordyline grew high,
dividing into a capital Y

when its weight became too much to be borne
by one trunk: dual trees growing side by side,
separate yet aligned, forging a peace
sign cradled by the crook where the wood split

in two but remained glued by sap and loops
of grain, a testament to sun and rain,
counting out the years in-between
its planting and when the day came to leave.

Wild Berries

for Ray Givans

On humid afternoons, mid September,
she teaches you how to pick junipers,
blackberries and your favourite, redcurrants.
Which ones to choose, which to leave on the branch,

avoiding those growing below the waist
or close to the road, where teenagers race
cars shaped like bullets, blood red and silver.
You scoop handfuls of fruit into wicker

baskets to be transmuted into jam
and sealed inside jars with lids tight as clams.
You sneak some while sweet perfume fills the house.
They burst like rain in the shell of your mouth.

Goodwinter

for Harry and Philip Arrell

A slow decade, a war of attrition
with a stubborn house plagued by falling slates
and rising damp until a concession:
we packed up dog, child, kipple … the whole state

of us in reinforced cardboard tea chests,
each one numbered in bold *Sharpie* cursive,
contents catalogued in a manifest
lest they arrived on the far side worse off

for being lugged around by muscular
uncles whose vigour did not flag or fail.
We beat a retreat by streets crepuscular
with red brick, willow and wandering quail

to a chocolate box house in a nice part
of town: safe, a stone's throw from patio
to the library, duck pond and sweetheart
promenade. Real life was simpatico

with our dreams for a change. So, we gathered
dog and daughter, scooped up jars of laughter
and flagons of tears. Before we scattered,
we wrote our names on the attic rafters.

Mayura

Late at night, the harsh shrieking of peacocks
caged in the nearby park

halts me cold in my back garden. The moon
snares me within a shaft

of cold yellow like fish in a bucket.
My shadow stretches tall

like the Colossus across a quiet
of charred soot towards

the back fence and beyond, outwards across
the golf course, where bunkers

ring like pools of glass with the major key
chime of hundreds of eyes

gazing from the galaxies. This moment
cannot last. In a blink,

a chariot train of cloud sweeps into
the concave, obscuring

the moon and setting me free. The peacocks
fall still. I am once more

locked within the present where the need for sleep
calls me inside to dream.

Symbiosis

Twin brothers, victims of the cruellest trick:
both blind, one half deaf, they forsook the stick
in favour of hooking crook around crook
and braving streets of wild dogs, sudden gusts
and kerbstones jagged like a werewolf's teeth.

Casually cavalier, two pioneers
forged unseen lines through a noisy city,
working in perfect synchronicity.
Deprived of certain senses, they made amends
by taking turns to pierce holes through the dark,

each half placing trust in the space where faith
took physical form as a guiding arm,
resting hand on wrist to confront the risk
of the other coming to any harm.

Threading The Light

It took thirty-six hours to bring you home
though it may have been more, and it may have been less;
a day and a half in the eye of the storm
of laughing gas and sheets scented with lemon zest.

Something was wrong from the off: a lost wedding ring,
a snippety shift nurse, several botched
epidurals and an afternoon spent watching
your stuttering heartbeat playing hopscotch

on a fuzzy screen. I split my time between
fetching naff sandwiches from the hospital canteen
and telling your mum everything would be alright
when all I wanted to do was thread first light

into your eyes, and slap first breath into your chest,
but the timing was so tight, and the space in the cleft
so slight that I nearly forgot, and I nearly lost faith
but nothing is ever truly lost; it is only misplaced.

Four:
The Silent Shore

Altiplano, 1958

You must have felt so far from home that day,
    stranded countless notches along the spine
    of the Peruvian plateau,
looking on as a posse of useless men –

better Bible scholars than mechanics –
    argued and bantered over a jack
    and a blown tyre
while a merciless sun baked acrylic paint

from the car bonnet, forcing you outside.
    Sick with pregnancy and hypoxic air,
    you were glad
of the zephyr tickling both calves beneath

a hand-stitched floral dress long since faded.
    The afternoon light had turned silken
    but the air was dry,
and the lozenge of a language you failed

to learn tasted bitter on your tongue, like dark
    chocolate or the sweat
    pooling on your top lip.
Displaced from a barren landscape where the trail

had ceased blazing, you gazed at a zigzag
    highway, on whose tip
    an uncertain future quivered
like a mirage: a father broken by war,

a husband in the shipyard and a garden
    turned to bedlam by a brood
    of rowdy children.
This fresh life of heartache and joy was waiting.

The Daily Crossword

for Mum

The letters are no longer placed inside
the boxes. They were once bang on target:
neat bullet holes all dead straight in a line;
each answer correct and proudly square set.

Her hand was once firm but her words now squirm.
A tremor has become her signature.
The crossword has changed. The spaces that yearn
to be filled now yield to a silent cure.

Somehow we muddle through. I read the clues,
and do my best job of trying to jog
her faltering memory. We both choose
to ignore the fact that she has been robbed

of her keenest skill. Between rounds of pills
and the next day's meal order she replies –
oh, the surprise, when she knows *d'Urberville*,
Analogue or *Shinto*, as if her eyes

still hold the light like a lamp glimpsed through mist.
More often than not, the right words are lost,
her eyes start to drift, and my kindest gift
is to complete the rows down and across

and say, "That's right," as if this can make up
for the countless books bought when I was ill,
the countless answers taught when I got stuck,
and all the other gaps she helped to fill.

Slow Theft

1.

One by one, you watch blinding lights blink off,
and listen to the building's laboured breathing
slow. Somewhere else, within concrete depths, a lift
descends to a disused floor then comes to rest.

The world tilts like a ship at sea. The night yaws,
drifts and stumbles as if on stilts. The sudden shift
makes your stomach twist but there is no relief
to be gleaned from a vending machine dispensing

rotten teeth and bad dreams. The ward realigns.
Night nurses – kindness, comfort and warmth defined –
ghost from bed to bed, plumping pillows
and resting heads, fending off fear and dread

while doctors whisper terms to which they defer
when there are no other words to prepare
for that for which we cannot be prepared.
It is quite the feeling to be balanced

on the prick of a needle: in a private
room she lies – light as a wish, thin as a sigh –
shrinking further each time I take the path
that winds from my front drive to her bedside.

2.

Home. A Margaret rose is choked in an overgrown
hedge. Some day, you will shear its gasping stem
and wrench it free. For now, its roots stretch too deep.
You leave it be and allow its vibrant colours
to be eclipsed by leaves. How could you decide
which is worse: let nature take its bitter course
or swallow the pill? In the car again, you watch
as a rainbow arcs across Craigantlet hills.

"Let go, my son," it says. "Be still. Be still."

The Switch

When I lost you, something fell loose,
came unfixed:

the thread that sewed me together
unpicked and unstitched;

a thin and icy fingertip clicked
a switch

right beside the one that was tripped
that night

my baby girl just about made it
after a glitch

in the system nearly stopped her heart
from beating

and all my heavy breathing failed
to pitch

more life onto the knife and gloves
two beats above

true love and the end of my wits.
She did not quit.

She fought and breathed and hollered
and kicked

and grasped tightly to the edge
of the cliff

between a life rich in fullness
and the abyss.

She clawed her way back with mettle
and grit

and has carried on in the same vein
ever since.

But when you aimed for the same light,
you missed.

Not even my surfeit of flitting breath
could fit

between the beats that your heart skipped,
and you slipped

between the bars when your faint pulse
went amiss.

Yes, the rest of us left behind laugh
and reminisce

but when she asks about where
I inherit

my sense of humour, as black
as liquorice,

and why I sometimes get mawkish,
my mood shifts

and I barely notice the switch.

Grief Is Great

i.m. Margaret Elizabeth Thompson

1. Sorrow

At first it feels like being stabbed: the knife
slides in and the breath slips out. This blade, honed
by childhood fear and carved from purest ice,
is never quite removed. A scar hides a wound
that bleeds, years after the fact, deep and wide

as the freezing lake into which you dive
each time you hear the creak on the top stair
that once bore their heel when they were alive.
Now, silence reminds you: they are not there.
Nor are they *here*. So, the fickle heart shrives

the reason why you cry while driving home,
cocooned by the heat of an empty car;
or sitting in the living room, alone,
where time pours like treacle, and slow blue hours
tumble face down like cemetery stones

in that overgrown graveyard you once found
by a church near Binevenagh. You tried
the door, half swallowed by the wind-burnt ground,
but it would not give, then peeped through half-pried
slats but there was no light to shade the sound

of your voice bouncing back as a stranger:
older, somehow, and shaped like an ellipse,
bruising between the cross and the manger –
the voice you heard streaming from your own lips
when you recited psalms as the danger

closed tight like bear claws. Echoes of echoes
haunt you now. They swell and shrink like cruel stars.
They recede then push back when the night throws
up a fist, southpaw, sucker punch, and powers
you to the floor. The waves come … the waves go.

2. Isolation

They say that grief is great, a shearing thing
that sears and sunders then disappears back
into its cave like a hibernating
bear, then wakes, cross as sticks, booming through cracks
in stone just like the untamed sea that brings

you in shady dream to the silent shore
to which you always drift when fog rolls in.
The storm transforms from a moan to a roar,
and your one-man boat, carried by the wind,
dashes upon the rocks of that forlorn

atoll, chained by coral, shaped like a scar,
sharp as a scimitar. Here, there is naught
but paper cuts, poppy bruises … a war
of salty crocodile tears that you blot
with nettles until your cheeks are red raw.

You return home but that minotaur grief
still waits patiently in his maze of bones,
knowing full well that in time you will cleave
to him again. That black labyrinth owns
a part of you that cannot be retrieved.

3. *Euphemism*

Loss: a strange word for this separation,
as if they had been misplaced like spare change
or left on the moon where all forsaken
things wait but can never be found again.

4. *Penthos*

Since then,
you wear your friend grief like a second skin.

There are days
when the doldrums descend without warning:

a blue curtain
of poisoned velvet that blocks out the sun.

You feel guilty
for those days when you dare to be happy,

as if to still love
or laugh is blasphemy, a disservice

to their memory,
and an acceptance that life must not wait.

You worry less
yet have entirely lost your confidence.

There are days
when all of your nerve endings are exposed,

screaming wildly,
as if lit on fire and pumping with blood,

and there are those
when you feel half-asleep, two or three beats

removed from a world
that will not stop for slowcoaches or those

still clutching
the hook where grief hangs you when it heads out.

5. *Lament*

If grief has a colour
      or dolour has a taste
then I could paint the shape
      of this weight pressing down

upon my chest: how loss
      cannot be tamed or named
or kept in check, slipped back
      into the deck once drawn.

6. *The Thread*

That memory: driving silently to the edge of town
by a road stretched like string between plastic cups,
too slack to carry the ailing signal from base to the place
you falsely call *the home*. She waits alone, watching the window

glow, from day to night, from sunshine to snow, curled up,
   childlike,

light as light itself, fumbling with the thread of things both said
and unsaid: what she will tell the boy who will darken
her door in half an hour, whose name she cannot recall

and whose face she does not quite recognise but whose eyes
are full of swimming pools and spaceships and dinosaurs
and *knock-knock* jokes. She half-remembers Peach Melba pokes
and trips to the sea, half-forgets sneaking gifts beneath

a Christmas tree. But when you arrive, she is asleep.
You sit on the sunken reclining seat. You tug
at your fraying cuffs while she falls further into her nest.
You hold your breath while her breath slows within her chest.

7. *Disremembering*

One arm in my raincoat, halfway through the door
when a penny clatters inside my skull:
        What are you doing? She is not there anymore.

A force of habit engrained firm as a scar,
        memory plays callous tricks with the senses,
taunts and teases the mind like the shore

does to the tide, like the wind does with rusted chimes
that discord on the corner of an abandoned house.

8. *Falling*

Unpegged,
        booted from the nest half-fledged,
you fear that that the fall
        may break both your legs.

The ledge has crumbled
and your grip has slipped.
The cord has been cut
and you plummet
into the crevasse,
praying to God
that the fall will not last
and yet you find a dry roof,
a warm bed
and bread laid on your table
like manna:
vestiges left by the departed dead,
those who led the way,
and wove a thread,
who paved a guide line
through wilderness,
squall
and frozen wastes.
It is a debt that you cannot repay.

9. *Marah*

Here, you find you have reached the lowest low:
grief, that pitiless beast, gives no quarter
but ties each tired limb to the Four Horses
of the Apocalypse ... and quarters you.

Escaping, you think you are in the clear
but predictably you hear hunting horns
and hot barks of dogs sniffing out your trail,
louder and more shrill than a banshee wail.

When they catch you, they drag you back to Hell:
     that freezing oubliette, a private cell
on whose walls are scratched the days expended
     since you first became locked inside this well

of sighs and vipers and a beam of light
     tuned to the frigid regard of the moon.

10. *Sabretooth*

That ancient beast grief, long since thought deceased,
reanimates and bares its razor teeth.

Those tapered sabres scratch your naked nape –
passive and yielding, longing to escape

the living snare in which you have been trapped –
but the wildcat throws you upon his back.

You steal through a thorny, moonlit terrain,
hands gripping fur, great paws' heavy refrain

startling wildlife as you ride to the sun,
your thundering heartbeats thrumming as one.

The journey is done. Light starts to creep
across the hills. The beast returns to sleep,

curls up in its cave, grants a brief reprieve
and you are set free but still not at peace.

11. *Bargaining*

for Sonia

Grief, that great revelator,
pulled you apart,
changed and recalibrated,

altered your very DNA,
then sewed you back together –
but in a different shape.

Grief split your atoms,
rent your very matter,
and the fallout

is still to dissipate.
Grief caused the bones of you
to ache, some cogs to spin

faster, and some to spin less.
It is relentless in its
intrusion. You wear grief like a brand,

a tattoo, a contusion,
a band of gold
or secret handshake

that allows you entrance
to a covert club,
a backstreet speakeasy

where they sell shots
of addictive liquor
with a noxious flavour.

You leave without drinking
and head home, sober,
hoping that grief
will not win you over.

12. *Unnesting*

So, the time comes to sell your childhood home.
You moonwalk through empty bedrooms that glow
like bowls of jewels, escaping the traces
of your own footsteps, built up over years

like compressed layers of rock. The unlit
fireplace, the shadow where a clock once hung,
imprints left by chairs like marks on damp grass –

how quickly the present becomes the past.

13. *Graphology*

Sorting all of her personal effects,
you find a notebook, stamped *Casterton School*,
once home to four of the Brontë sisters

whose novels you box up for donating
to charity shops she liked to frequent.
Inside, the clean, dry pages bear witness

to a textbook lesson in penmanship.
Her script, one stroke away from Garamond,
is schoolteacher neat: the sterns and brackets

hugging tight to the baseline like a dog
orbiting its master's heel; the open
bowls like a mouth reciting poetry

or crooning Elvis Presley; the cursive
precisely joined like a parent holding
a child for safety or comfort. Browsing

her jottings, slightly faded, and scaling
her ascenders as a toddler might climb
a make-believe stalk, you can bear the weight

of her letters and the touch of her hand.

14. *The Upward Turn*

Here is where you pull out the blade
        and learn to live with the hole it made.

It is not so much a letting go
        as an act of survival. You know

that time will not halt nor leave you behind
        but will swaddle you in the soft kind

of numbness that comes as a blessing.
        It may not ease the pain nor lessen

the sting but brings a tender *quid pro quo*:
        grief is the channel through which love flows.

Consider the wind through strong branches,
        the sea, the weight of winter blankets,

those hymns, the taste of freshly picked fruit,
       the crunch of gravel beneath your boots,

how light pours like syrup on the sill.
       Grief is great but love is greater still.

15. *Hope*

Surely, you know that there is always hope:
a love song, a rainbow or a photo
of a young girl, slim and tanned and smiling

at an unseen camera capturing
a fleeting glimpse of life at its sweetest,
glistering, as if viewed from the open

window of a speeding car, rocketing
along the thread that divides and borrows
all our yesterdays and all our tomorrows.

Five:
Reaching Out

Fraternity

At first light, a ramshackle bus bundles
up a carriageway that winds through shark tooth
Dolomites, high above a lake stretched flat
and peppered with windsurfers patiently

waiting for the day's Pelèr to pick up
speed. They shrink to coloured daubs, glittering
strips of paper peeling from a mirror
that gives back a glowing ball of shy sun.

Passengers slumber in drowsy summer,
skin still pricked by ultraviolet and zinc
oxide, bellies still full of limoncello.

In the back seat, two young brothers cradle
one another in the cool blue morning
of the day's first imaginings, curled up

like wolf cubs, sapping heat from each other
in the yearning absence of their mother.

Sleeptown

for Francis Jones

Beneath an implausibly wide pastel blue sky
on the first weekend of an Orbison summer
spent in a yesteryear coastal town, trapped in time,
we fritter our loose change on tuppeny nudgers

then take a whirl on the carousel, the ghost train
and big dipper. After, we assault smiling lips
with pokes of vinegary chips and swigs of Maine
Brown Lemonade. Later, as a melting sun dips

behind a dyed pink tide, we walk the strand, hand hooked
in hand, past the keening revival tent, our skin
salted by a sea stolen from a storybook.
We may not have diners, rolleramas, drive-ins

and Wurlitzers stacked with teenage dreams and silver
string but there are spaceship rides for half a shilling
and frozen tastes of Italy from the parlour.
We may not drive Cadillacs but we live like kings.

Homecoming

It is the pleasing movement of door key
sliding inside lock, the click of barrel
turning and ball bearings retracting
into place, the echo of patio

as outer and inner door are unfixed
from their jambs. It is each handle's weight, shape
and grain that meets your palm like a greeting,
like a rough-hewn handshake from an old friend.

It is the scuff of varnished wood across
carpet, the console table, letter rack
and ghostglow of standard lamps in the hall,
the radiators' contented ticking

after clocking off for the night, fading
embers in hearth, hothouse smell of kitchen.
It is a return to how each day starts
and ends by slipping into bed with you.

On Castlerock Beach

for Anna

Years from now, when I have long since whispered
into the air, you might wake in the dead
of night and reach for a glass of water
to quench the sandbank of thirst that has swept

into your mouth. And, as if by magic,
a baroque pearl will roll into your palm
as a memory forms like spit and dirt:
that time when you, the guts of four, chirruped

with glee as we three, bare feet and short sleeves,
scoured the whole stretch of the strand for sea glass
where forks of lightning had frozen the sand.
And how we squealed when one, two, five and eight

raindrops grazed our skin just before a freak
downpour blurred the shore and turned the sea sky
into a frayed hem. In a shower of gems
you snuzzled your mother's neck while we pegged

it to the car. The shower turned to a storm
while we, wet as the day that we were born,
peeled off clumps of clothes and cranked up the heat,
and nestled you into your toddler seat.

But here's something that you won't remember:
while your mum fished out wine gums
I beat a frenzied drum to the Bar Mouth
to retrieve the tiny pink shoe that dropped

from my pocket in all the commotion.
There, barely within reach on the swelling
beach, it was, helpless, taunted by the ocean.
For a moment it was almost claimed but

I picked it up and closed the gap between
what is God's and what is mine. Close behind,
the water rushed in and out of the void,
as if to say, "Next time ... next time ... next time."